ACE IT, AND BE HIRED!

Your Ultimate Guide To Ace The Job Interview - Every Time!

Judy S. Berman

Table of Contents

INTRODUCTION

CHAPTER TWO: SUCCESSFUL INTERVIEWS

CHAPTER THREE: THE HIRING PROCESS

CHAPTER FOUR: MASTERING INTERVIEW SKILLS

CHAPTER FIVE: PLANNING AND PREPARATION

CHAPTER SIX: DO'S AND DON'TS

CHAPTER SEVEN: QUESTIONS GUIDE

CHAPTER EIGHT: PUTTING IT ALL TOGETHER

CHAPTER NINE: QUESTIONS AND ANSWERS

CONCLUSION

INTRODUCTION

The importance of interviews

Imagine that you have recently been seeking employment. A call for an interview appears today. As you read the letter, how would you feel? ecstatic, energized, and eager to depart? Or on the other hand, uneasy, giving up to your fate, and defeated with a sense of impending ruin? Does the ensuing depiction appear to reflect how you would feel? Having a pessimistic attitude on your prospects, undervaluing your skills and expertise, and convincing yourself that you will not succeed? Maybe that's how you've reacted in the past when you've been invited to interviews. Anything but cognitively dismissing your chances of succeeding will make that gloomy assumption come true.

If you get the chance to interview, you should be happy and excited. Isn't this the reason you initially applied for the position?

After all, you applied for the position because you wanted the opportunity to show the company that you were the finest candidate. You made all the effort necessary during the application process because you desired the job. Since it is quite uncommon to be given a job offer without first having a job interview, getting an interview moves you one step closer to your objective. However, you are not the only one who shudders at the idea of having to present yourself to a possible employer.

We all share the concern that we won't come across favorably while under examination, and we all worry that we'll put ourselves through the stress and effort of preparing for nothing since we won't have much of a chance of getting the job in the first place. Such unfavorable views are the kiss of death for every job interview. There is a chance that you will go into the interview thinking you are a loser if you arrive feeling insecure.

Interviewers will pick up on a bad attitude right away.

They are aware of uneasy and uneasy candidates and are less likely to be impressed by them than they are by those who appear more at ease and confident in themselves.

Isn't it time you learned how to exert more control when pushing yourself forward if you're interested in moving forward in your profession, getting promoted, and changing jobs? It is possible to alter the worrying and failing patterns from the past. You don't need to continue stumbling into the same traps that you have been. This book teaches you how to achieve these changes in your own life by transforming your natural anxieties and worries into tenacity and dynamism.

CHAPTER ONE: THE INTERVIEW PROCESS

INTERVIEW DEFINED

When looking for a career change, employers may ask you to participate in the interview process to understand your character traits, skills and attitude to work. Interviews allow an employer or interviewer to decide whether you are a suitable candidate for a vacant position. Learning more about interviews and how to present yourself during an interview can increase your chances of getting hired for a desirable job.

An interview is a discussion or conversation between a potential employer and a candidate. It is a selection process designed that helps an employer understand the skills, scrutinize their personality and character traits and check the domain knowledge. In this formal meeting, the employer asks questions to get information from a candidate. Usually, interviews happen during the last phase of the recruitment process and help companies select a suitable candidate for a job role. During an interview, the interviewer may ask you about their salary expectation, whereas you can ask about the job responsibilities.

Another purpose an interview serves is that it helps in authenticating a candidate's application. Employers use this opportunity to investigate a candidate's claim and check whether they can prove their claims.

Types Of Interviews

Structured interviews

A structured interview process is where an employer asks a fixed set of questions to all candidates appearing for an interview. Rather than focusing on experience-based questions, an employer prefers asking a fixed set of questions and recording the responses of every candidate. They grade these responses against a suitable scoring system and hire candidates based on this result. A structured interview is beneficial for both interviewers and candidates because it eliminates biases from the recruitment process.

Unstructured interviews

In unstructured interviews, a conversation occurs conversationally and spontaneously. The interviewer can ask questions related to a candidate's skills, experience, or qualifications. Such interviews do not follow any set format and the interview can go in any direction. It is a traditional interviewing method that organizations use to hire suitable candidates. Using an unstructured interview, interviewers gauge a candidate's interview skills by comparing their performance to other candidates.

Situational interviews

In a situational interview, employers present a candidate with a problem. Employers use this interview process to evaluate their approach to solving problems. Through such interviews, an employer understands what action a candidate would take in various job-related situations. When answering such questions, employers expect a candidate to give answers related to similar situations a candidate handled in the past.

Behavioral interviews

Behavioral interviews are a technique which employers use to gauge and evaluate a candidate's past behavior in different situations. It helps in understanding how a candidate would perform in similar situations at work. It is easier for an employer to predict the success of a candidate on their past performance. Usually, the employer asks open-ended questions about specific situations to hire a suitable candidate. The employer then tallies a candidate's response against an anchored rating scale.

Stress interviews

Employers gauge a candidate's ability to respond to stress in different workplace situations using this interview style. For some job roles like consulting, employers conduct stress interviews to spot sensitive applicants and separate high-stress tolerance candidates from the rest. It is a great interview style to find sensitive applicants who may lose their calm attitude in stressful situations. In such interviews, employers create anxiety to see the reaction of a candidate.

Technical interviews

A technical interview is an interview type that helps an employer understand technical and job-related aptitude. When applying for healthcare, information technology, engineering, and science, a candidate is more likely to face technical interviews. Through such interviews, an employer gauges your technical expertise and it helps in understanding whether you have the skills required to complete your job-specific duties.

One-to-one interviews

It is a common type of interview where only one interviewer interviews a candidate. It is a conversational type of interview where the employer drives the agenda initially and a candidate asks questions toward the end. Usually, an employer may ask general, technical, situational, and behavioral questions in a one-to-one interview. It is a great interview technique to understand a candidate's experience and domain knowledge.

Video or phone interviews

Such interviews occur on the phone or via video. An employer conducts such interviews when a candidate cannot attend a face-to-face interview. Rather than calling every candidate for an interview, employers usually conduct phone interviews to screen potential candidates. When candidates receive an unexpected call from employers, they give spontaneous answers that help an employer understand the candidate's intelligence and interpersonal skills.

Types Of Interviews Formats

When preparing for an interview, researching different interview formats can help you prepare better for your upcoming interview. Here are different interview formats:

Individual

Individual interview formats involve only one interviewer with one candidate. In such interviews, employers can ask situation or behavioral questions. Usually, in such questions, an interviewer may ask the following questions:
Job-specific questions help an interviewer understand whether a candidate is a good fit.

General interview questions related to experience, background, strength, and qualification.
When going for an individual interview, focus on highlighting your relevant skills and solving problems for the company. Also, answer questions by providing examples from your previous job experience.

Group

In group interviews, a company interviews multiple applicants at the same time. The interviewer may provide a topic for the group to discuss. During their discussion, an observer rates their performance. Such an interview format helps an employer understand the differences and nuances in the skills and qualifications of candidates. It helps employers test a candidate's interpersonal and communication skills. Usually, in group interviews, interviewers can understand how candidates apply their skills, strengths, and qualifications when interacting with others.

Panel

In a panel interview, several interviewers assess an individual's candidate on their skills, qualification, and experience. Often, the panel comprises a hiring manager, a colleague, or a team manager. In such a format,
Interviewers usually ask questions in succession. The answer a candidate provides allows a panel to see how they fit the company's values and culture. During a panel interview, focus on maintaining eye

contact with everyone and share your success with them.

Multiple-round

When hiring for a technical role, many organizations conduct multiple interviews to evaluate candidates' skills and qualifications. In multiple-round interviews, the first two rounds may comprise a technical round. The last round may be with a hiring manager to discuss the candidature and salary expectations. Success in multiple-round interviews involves applying communication and interpersonal skills to answer questions that highlight your skills.

Informational

The informational interview format is where you interact with a professional working in a company you are preparing for. In an information interview, candidates contact professionals from different companies and schedule a time to meet them. A professional can help in understanding the work culture and environment of the company. They answer questions about different job roles and potential growth in the company. When going for an informational interview, prepare a list of questions you want to ask about the company and its culture.

Computer-assisted

Often, computer-assisted interviews are video interviews. Employers provide a series of questions on their screen by pressing the key on the keyboard. Though this technique results in faster hiring, it cannot assess a candidate's emotional intelligence, communication skills, or interpersonal skills. Companies prefer using this interview technique when screening and filtering out a large base of candidates applying for a single job.

Why do interviews take place?

Interviews are held to gather information and to appraise character. In an interview for a job, the employer first selects those applicants who seem worth interviewing. The next step is to find out which of the shortlisted candidates (those chosen for interview) would be the most suitable person for the job.

If I asked you to find out about somebody whom you had never met before, you would probably choose to talk to that person face to face. Interviews are just a common-sense way for people to meet, find out about each other, and ask each other questions. So, as well as the employer seeing you, you also have the chance to make your own decisions about the employer, the job on offer, and the type of organization or company concerned.

If you are selected to come for an interview there is every chance that you could end up getting the job. The employer likes what you have said about yourself so far and wants to know more about you.

CHAPTER TWO: SUCCESSFUL INTERVIEWS

11 Tips For A Successful Interview

You've spent hours revising your resume, tweaking your cover letter, and practicing your pitch. You've made a list of your top five target companies and finally landed an interview with your #1 choice. SUCCESS.

But now you've got a couple of days to prepare for an interview and you're completely overwhelmed! It is time to do your homework. Use these 11 simple tips for a successful interview to help you land that dream job.

Tip #1: Do your research.

Having little or no knowledge of the company is the most common mistake job seekers make during interviews. Interviewing is just plain hard if you have no idea what the company does!

To that end, researching the company thoroughly before the interview is our most important interview tip for success. Check out the company's website, recent news articles online, social media channels, and whatever else you can find. The goal is to gain a working knowledge of the company's services, values, and culture, as well as the competitive landscape. That way, you'll be in a better

position to sell yourself; you have a chance to think through which of your qualities or experiences could help them meet their goals should you be hired.

If you know the names of the individuals with whom you will be meeting, take it a step further and look them up on LinkedIn. This will give you an understanding of their background and common areas of interest between yourself and the interviewer.

Don't worry: you won't be expected to know everything about a company or a position during an interview. But the more you know, the better.

Tip #2: Be prepared.

Bring a folder or portfolio with extra copies of your resume, a copy of professional references, any examples of past work (if applicable), and a pad of paper and a pen to take notes during the interview. Before your interview, make sure you have the correct interview location and look up directions to the location. This will help avoid unnecessary stress on the day of the interview.

Tip #3: Dress to impress.

It's time to get out your best interview clothes! In most instances, we recommend wearing a suit. Even if the company for which you are interviewing has a casual or laid-back environment, you don't want to give the appearance that you are coming into the interview casual, so dress to impress and look confident!

Tip #4: Arrive EARLY.

NEVER arrive late for an interview. Always arrive at the interview location at least 5 to 10 minutes before the interview.

Tip #5: Exude confidence

Employers are always on the lookout for a firm handshake and eye contact to gauge confidence. During the interview, speak confidently (even though you may be nervous on the inside). Smiling, nodding when the interviewer is speaking, and having a solid posture all send positive signals to interviewers.

Do your best to avoid playing with objects, fidgeting, looking around the room, and chewing gum. This type of body language can give the interviewer the impression that you are disengaged.

Tip #6: LISTEN.

We often hear from our clients that one of the most neglected interview skills displayed by candidates during their interview is a lack of listening. Listening is very important as it allows you to answer the interviewer's questions accurately. Listen to questions being asked of you and respond with detailed and concise responses.

Tip #7: Share specific examples.

Before the interview, take some time to reflect on your career path. Prepare examples that highlight your successes to help you create a story for the employer. Remember, your past behavior is a strong indicator of your future performance.

Put yourself in the interviewer's shoes and determine certain questions you think they may ask you. Then, develop answers to those questions that include performance metrics whenever possible, or specific supporting details.

Tip #8: Show interest by asking questions.

Nothing will get you shown the door quicker than a 'take it or leave it' attitude. If the interviewer doesn't feel like you want the job, you won't get it. Period. The Undercover Recruiter found that failing to ask for the job is the most common mistake made by interviewers.

You can show interest by commenting on remarks made by the interviewers, or—even easier—by asking questions. You can prepare questions ahead of time, leaving less need for on-the-fly thinking.

On top of that, it is a big turnoff for employers when candidates don't ask questions during or after the interview. This is your opportunity to find out valuable information from the employer firsthand, so don't miss your shot.

Tip #9: Be positive.

Companies want to hire people with positive attitudes. This is not the time to sound off on how horrible your last boss was, or how terrible the coffee was at your last job. The interviewer will be trying to uncover how you handle adversity, so do your best to put everything in the best possible light and focus on the positive in negative situations.

Tip #10: Be yourself.

All of these tips for interviews that we've mentioned must be balanced out by the importance of being yourself in the interview. Don't spend your time trying to prepare for what you think they want to hear. The main purpose of an interview is for the potential employer to learn more about you and figure out if you're a good fit for the role. In fact, the question that is most likely to be asked is 'Tell me about yourself.'

Your resume has already shown that you have the background to be successful in the job, so be confident in your achievements and skills. If you fake your way through an interview, you may find yourself in a role in which you can never truly be successful.

Tip #11: Follow up with a thank-you note.

Within 24 hours, send a thank-you email or card. This message is another opportunity to remind the interviewer of all the positive traits you possess that you can bring to this position and company. If you don't send one, another candidate probably will. Wouldn't you prefer to keep the odds stacked in your favor?

The thank-you note is just one of many post-interview tactics to set yourself apart from other interviewees. Here's how to nail the post-interview process.

An interview is an opportunity to sell yourself to an employer on your experience, personality, and what you can bring to the table for the desired position. The majority of the time, the most qualified candidate is not the one who is hired. It typically is the candidate that does the best job selling themselves to the employer and showcasing their fit within the job and company.

By following these tips for a successful interview, you are on the right path to landing your dream job.

POINTS TO REMEMBER

✓ Do not turn down an interview because you are afraid

✓ Be positive

✓ Prepare, Prepare, and Prepare

✓ Make eye contact

✓ Be confident and be calm

✓ Never anticipate failure

CHAPTER THREE: THE HIRING PROCESS

What employees seek for in a candidate

Your cover letter and resume have earned you an interview because the potential employer has seen things in your education, training, and experience that make you an attractive candidate. The next step is the interview process. No matter the type of interview you face—individual, group, or panel—there are specific things interviewers look for to help them determine your ultimate suitability to fill an open position.

Your body language

The first impression you'll make in your in-person or virtual interview is how you appear and what your body language says about you. In addition to being neat and orderly in appearance, present a relaxed but alert demeanor. Maintain eye contact and a friendly smile and use hand gestures when appropriate. Eye contact can feel uncomfortable or impossible for some, but other nonverbal cues can help project your confidence or demonstrate your interest in the role.

Likeability

Think about the characteristics you appreciate in people you like, and then do your best to exhibit those traits in your interview. In addition to being polite, show that you are easy to get along with and cooperative.

Openness to new approaches

Your potential employer may be impressed by your past performance, but they also want to know that you are open to trying new ways of doing things. Be sure to communicate that you are flexible in your thinking and willing to try new approaches and new solutions.

Preparation

Interviewers appreciate it when you're well prepared because it gives them a preview of your readiness for work if hired. Have all collateral materials you may need, like copies of your resume, reference letters, and portfolio of work examples, if appropriate. Have a pen, pad, or notebook handy, and ensure your phone is silenced.

Soft skills in action

Your interview is the perfect time to demonstrate your soft skills. Empathy, integrity, dependability, creativity, and adaptability are all skills you can embody during the interview process.

Leadership

Mention examples of times you took charge and provided good leadership. If you volunteered for assignments, assumed leadership in a group setting, or led a project, share those experiences with your interviewer.

Confidence

Believe in yourself and behave accordingly. Let your interviewer know that you recognize your value and are excited to be able to share it as you learn from others.

Passion

Interviewers want to find people who are passionate about their work. Share your enthusiasm about your skills and talents, and communicate your professional dreams and ambitions.

Success stories

Interviewers look for the potential for future successes by hearing your stories of past successes. Be prepared to talk about your previous successes, whether in personal undertakings, past work situations, or as a student or trainee. Know your accomplishments on the job or in your personal life, and share them if appropriate.

Curiosity

An interview is also your chance to ask questions. Engaged applicants are curious about the hiring process and ask things like:
Why is this position needed?
How will you know that you hired the right person?
How does this role fuel the company's overall success?
What immediate challenges and opportunities await the person who fills this role?
What are the three key things you're looking for in the person who will have this job?

Personality

One of the most important things is to be yourself. Your interviewer needs to get a sense of the authentic you to judge your fit with your prospective team and the company culture. Instead of thinking of playing a role in your interview to get the job, envision the interview as an opportunity to show off your best self.

Thoughtfulness

How thoughtful you are while asking and answering questions in your interview can show the hiring manager your critical-thinking skills. If you need additional information to answer a question, ask the hiring manager to clarify so you can deliver a thorough answer. You can also explain your thought process as you work through a solution to give them a more in-depth perspective of your thoughtfulness.

Self-direction

Let your interviewer know your thoughts on where you currently are on your career path. Discuss where you have been, where you are presently, and where you'd like to be as your career progresses. This helps the interviewer determine how you can move within the company.

Expectations

Let your interviewer know your expectations to ensure they align with the company. Communicate your thoughts about the role you've applied for and what you expect from the company.

Self-awareness

Be prepared to discuss your opinions about your work, citing your strengths and areas for improvement. Let your interviewer know that you want to be an active participant in your career.

Motivation

Let your interviewer know that you are committed to taking on the role's challenges and look forward to joining the company. Interviewers want to understand why this role is essential to you, what motivates you to work for this company, and what level of self-motivation you bring with you.

Willingness

Your interview is an opportune time to showcase your willingness to be a team player and an effective employee. Interviewers respond positively when prospective employees ask, "How can I help?" Being eager to be of service is a valuable attribute you can highlight. Your willing attitude could be the determining factor in getting the job.

Understanding of the company

If there are two candidates for a position who are equally qualified, the one with a better understanding of the company will likely get the job. As you prepare for your interview, research the following aspects of the company:

Providing proof that you are the right candidate

If you have been called for an interview, there is no reason why you should not be the person who eventually gets offered the job. You stand just as much chance of being successful as any of the other candidates to be interviewed. How you have positioned yourself so far has worked. The way you described yourself on the paper application has appealed to the employer and you are amongst the front runners to get the job. To capitalise on your success so far, you must research thoroughly exactly what you put in your CV or application form. The mixture of your background and your current situation has appealed to the person short-listed for the interview.

 proof that you are the right candidate

Let us consider the interview situation for a moment. What is happening there? A strange situation has been set up – we do not normally have to talk to total strangers about our personal details but in a job interview we have to divulge everything about our background, experiences, and personality to the employer. This situation arises because the employer has something that we want – the job – and we are 'on show' to convince them that we are the most suitable candidate for that job. The best candidate on the day may not be the one with the longest experience or the widest set of skills, as this could be ascertained from a simple comparison of the application forms.

It will be the person who seems to fit in best and is most impressive on the day of the interview and this is why your whole performance will be taken into account when the decision about who to give the job to is made.

Employers have to make their decision based on three areas relevant to any job:

- *Your qualifications and skills – what you know and what you can do.*

- *Your experience and work background – where you have been and what you have done;*

- *Your personality and character – who you are and how you behave.*

The most important of these is the last one. Candidates may fall short of the advertised skills and qualifications for a job and often too lack the required experience but still manage to convince the employer that they are the best candidate on offer. How? By stressing that they have the right personality to fit into the organization and contribute fully to the fortunes of that company. Skills can be taught and experience can be gained once in the job if necessary – but one's personality cannot be changed so easily.

In a competitive job market where there may be many competent candidates for every job, satisfying these three bullet points (page 19) are the minimum required for possible employment. When several able and experienced candidates are in front of an interview panel they will make their decision based on two more factors:

If you can convey a sense that you can 'own' this job and look after the part of the business it concerns, you will come over as a very valuable addition to the organization. No employer wants a new person at work who has to have their hand held for the first three months of their employment. This would be just too much of a drain and a responsibility and represents a major investment of time and trouble. Employers want you to be able to come in, settle in, and get stuck in straight away with the minimum of fuss and effort.

CHAPTER FOUR: MASTERING INTERVIEW SKILLS

Top 14 Skills employers look for in a candidate

During interviews, employers are trying to uncover your skills and how they relate to a position. Knowing how to answer skills-based questions demonstrates that you have the experience and knowledge to deliver results in a role and can help you stand out from the competition.

Let's dive into the importance of practicing for interviews, why employers ask skills interview questions and the most important skills you should mention during an interview.

Why do interviewers ask skills questions?

Many companies now use automation in their initial screening process, which means software scans resume or applications for key terms to determine if a candidate meets the minimum criteria for a job. But saying that you have the skills required to get to the interview round, and actually having relevant experience are two very different things.
If you want to hone your interview skills and get more job offers, you first have to master the art of explaining how you have used a skill to achieve a result. That, in turn, helps the interviewer evaluate your suitability for the role, your strengths and weaknesses, and how you might fit within the team.

Determine suitability for the role

The main reason for asking skills questions is to learn whether or not a job seeker is a good fit for the role. If you poured over the job description and researched the company before the interview, it should be easy to answer these questions since most employers include the specific skills relevant to their roles in the job post.

To impress the interviewer, make sure your answers mention the soft and hard skills relevant to the role. Back your responses with real-life examples of situations where your skills helped deliver results for your employer.

For example, many job seekers embellish their foreign language abilities and suggest they are conversational or fluent in a language when they really just took a few classes in high school. Someone who is truly fluent and can use a language in a business setting could offer an example, "I negotiated three contracts in Mandarin, totaling $3.5 million in value for my last company.

Identify your strengths and weaknesses

Employers can also use skills-related interview questions to assess strengths and weaknesses relative to the position. As a candidate, you should determine the essential skills required for the role, and craft your answers to position yourself as the ideal person for the job.
If you're applying for a sales position, the skills you should mention in the interview might include applicable software programs you've used in managing your client base or negotiation skills. Be prepared with quantifiable data on how you have used those skills to meet or exceed goals.

The best way to answer questions about your weaknesses is to contextualize how you manage them—or like to be managed—to perform effectively. That can also help the interviewer and hiring manager determine if you'll be a natural addition to the team. If you're easily distracted by the constant ping of instant messages and email alerts, that might mean explaining that you need blocks of uninterrupted time to produce your best work.

Determine if you're a cultural fit

Employers need to gauge if you would succeed within the organization. A candidate should have the right mix of personal, fundamental, and teamwork skills. If you're an extrovert applying to a company that prioritizes individual contributors over teams, you may not be a great culture fit—and that's okay. Culture needs to be a fit for both the company and the candidate, so this can also be an opportunity for them to learn more about how the company operates.

Top skills to mention during an interview.

Communication

Excellent communication skills are vital in any job. Your answers should demonstrate your ability to deliver information clearly and concisely. Talk about verbal and nonverbal communication skills relevant to the role, including writing, active listening, and presentation skills.

Business acumen

Show off your knowledge of the industry, as well as your understanding of the organization's mission and vision, the markets it serves, the competition, and the strategies for generating revenue. Business acumen or commercial awareness skills are especially vital in sales and other customer-facing positions. Researching the company will turn up insights that will help you use this skill to your advantage in an interview.

Collaboration or teamwork

Teamwork and collaboration skills are also vital for success in any position, especially for roles that require working as part of a team. Most roles require regular work with fellow contributors. Emphasize your ability to build and maintain positive working relationships for the benefit of the organization.

Adaptability

Employers value highly-adaptable employees, and they succeed in a wide range of roles and instinctively pivot to find solutions when situations call for them. In fast-changing business environments, flexible workers help their organizations turn roadblocks into opportunities.

Problem-solving

Companies value employees who can solve problems because they can identify potential opportunities before others. Great problem-solvers make outstanding leaders because they are adept at helping the company manage difficult situations. These employees take initiative, are innovative, and understand their organization's vision.

Positivity

Optimistic employees are assets to their companies because they learn from setbacks and use challenges to grow and support their peers and organization.

Organization

An organized employee can prioritize effectively, work efficiently, and meet deadlines. Interview skills answers about the organization should highlight how you manage time and prioritize projects.

Leadership

Whether you are applying for an entry, middle, or senior role, employers love employees who can lead others. Leadership skills include the ability to delegate, assign tasks, set deadlines, motivate and support, and provide constructive feedback to colleagues and team members.

Negotiation

Negotiation and persuasion skills are essential in roles related to sales and customer service. A good negotiator should have solid communication and interpersonal skills and a deep understanding of the industry.

Confidence

When talking about confidence, it is important to be assertive without sounding arrogant. Emphasize your ability to make decisions and own them.

Perseverance

Companies want workers who can confront challenges without losing focus. Your answer should demonstrate you can persevere and dedicate your skills and strength to the company during hard times.

Self-motivation

Self-motivated people rarely quit before they get results. Self-motivators require less of their managers' attention to finish projects.

Ability to work under pressure

The ability to work under pressure shows you can deliver in less-than-ideal situations, and you won't lose your focus or become overwhelmed. If you are applying for a role in a high-stress or fast-moving industry, this skill is essential.

IT skills

Most jobs require at least basic IT skills, including the ability to use and trouble-shoot documents, spreadsheet software, and social media tools. Explain how you used IT skills and tools in previous roles, using real-life examples to support your answer.

Even when you're not actively looking, it's important to keep practicing good interview skills. You never know when your dream job might come up, so stay prepared.

CHAPTER FIVE: PLANNING AND PREPARATION

Interview preparation tips

Job interviews are nerve-wracking. It doesn't matter if you've done one or 15 — they rarely get easier.

One survey found that 93% of Americans experienced anxiety from job interviews. And within that survey, 41% said what made them most nervous was being unable to answer a difficult question.

But we can prepare for our job interviews, which should limit our job interview nerves. Interview preparation will help you become more comfortable and knowledgeable during the hiring process. You can confidently answer common interview questions rather than fumbling or trying to wing them. Of course, it takes time and dedication to know how to prepare for an interview, but that's why we're here.

Strong interviewing skills don't happen overnight. We'll explain the best ways to prepare for an interview by making your first impression count and giving yourself plenty of prep time beforehand. Let's start at the beginning and discuss the first step to wow your potential employer.

The first step on your job search journey

You know how to prepare for things. When you're going for a walk and you notice some dark clouds, you bring an umbrella. It's a good habit, so why not practice something similar in interviews?

Whether you're changing jobs or trying to do some career planning, interview prep is a key part of your journey. It helps take out some nerves and allows you to complete your interview knowing you put in the work. And you won't accomplish your career aspirations without acing a few interviews, so today's effort will pay off in the future.

Your interview preparation will include:

Gaining as much knowledge of the company as possible

Try looking on the company website, check their social media, or do your best to network. When you take the time to prepare, you're filling your brain with tips and skills that'll help you during the whole interview process.

Even knowing about the company culture will give you a clue as to how you'd fit in and contribute.

Knowing the details of the role you're applying for

If the hiring manager asks a question like why you want to work there, you'll be prepared to include details about the company and speak confidently in your answer. You'll have insight into what problem-solving questions you might be asked or how your skills will impact the team.

Reviewing your experience and strengths and weaknesses. Any interview will probably include a scenario question where you can draw on previous jobs to explain what you'd do and why it'd be effective. Are you responsible for managing a high volume of tasks on short deadlines? What helps you succeed at that? Make sure you know so you're ready to share.

Interview preparation boosts your chances of succeeding in your interview and ultimately landing the job. But let's dive in to explain what specific action to take to prepare.

Interview prep stretches far beyond just researching the company. Some preparation tips don't have to do with the job itself and instead focus on your mind and body.

Others are practical and help you knock on the right door when the time comes.

You can do a lot to prepare for an interview, so we've compiled a list of 15 interview preparation tips for you to read:

Dedicate time to craft your resume

Your potential employer doesn't want to see typos or grammatical errors in your resume. Make your resume stand out and ensure it's clean and organized.

Practice some relaxation techniques
Calm yourself down before your interview so you have a clear mind. Studies have found that envisioning success and shifting your

focus to something productive helps ease interview nerves.

Do some mock interviews
A mock interview with friends or family will help you slip into the zone. You can practice discussing your work experience and career goals professionally and concisely.

Have a positive attitude:
The hiring manager isn't looking to fail you. Enter your interview with a positive mindset, and trust the hard work you've put in before to prepare. Your positivity might be infectious and help create a strong first impression.

Plan your route accordingly

The last thing you want to be is late.
   Think about how you'll travel to arrive promptly for your interview time. If it's a remote interview, make sure you've updated your video conferencing software and are in the meeting a few minutes early.

Have confident body language

Body language is integral to nonverbal communication. Make sure you have a firm handshake, make eye contact, sit up straight, and don't fidget.

Make a checklist of things you need

If you need to bring a reference list or portfolio, make sure they're ready to go and polished upon submitting your application. It's also a good idea to bring copies of your resume in case anyone wants to read it and for your reference.

Rest yourself the night before

Getting a proper amount of sleep the night before will help you wake up feeling energized. Take some time to relax the night before, and make time for it.

Write a list of your strengths

If you find it difficult to talk about yourself, prepare a list of things you're proud of ahead of time. Write down your skill sets, accomplishments, or certifications so you don't draw a blank at the moment.

Plan your outfit the night before

On the morning of your interview, you don't want to frantically rummage through your closet looking for the best outfit. Think of what you'd like to wear ahead of time and make sure it's clean and ready to go.

Turn off your electronics

Silence any alarms or notifications you have that might go off during your interview. You don't want any interruptions or things that might interrupt your focus.

Prepare a list of questions

After you've answered all the questions you've been asked, it's your turn to ask the hiring manager some questions. This is your opportunity to talk to your potential employer about salary expectations or learn more about the job itself. It also makes you seem more interested in the company.

Be assertive and polite

Practice ahead of time how you'll be polite but assertive when presenting yourself. Rather than being passive and hiding away, practice how you'll be bold and confident.

Think hard about your word choice

Recruiters won't be wowed if you use generic words they've heard hundreds of times before. Think of descriptive action verbs to help you stand out and make an impression.

Sharpen your listening skills

Listening carefully to each question will help you answer exactly how the hiring manager wants. Practice slowing things down and not rushing yourself with your answer as you listen to what people say. Use the words from their question when you're formulating your answer.

If you need extra interview tips specific to you, consider meeting with a BetterUp coach. They'll keep you focused on preparing for your interview and help you feel comfortable as you land your next job.

Importance of planning and preparation

Imagine that you have applied for a job you very much want. Today, 'plop', on to the doormat, comes a letter inviting you for an interview. Congratulations! So far everything you have done has impressed the employer. Now that we have more of an idea of the principles behind the interviewing process, we can look in more detail at what to say. PLANNING and **_PREPARATION_** allow you to immerse yourself in the process to give you **_CONFIDENCE_** which leads to **_ENTHUSIASM_** and **_SUCCESS_**.

An essential part of your preparation for attending any interview is deciding in advance your view of yourself, how you see the employer, and your ideas about what you will do in the job. This is particularly important if you are being asked to give a presentation as part of the interview. This part of the process of getting ready for an interview could be called research and development: research about the job and how you view it and development of your plan to depict yourself and your strengths.

Your view of yourself

Spend some time thinking about your employment history, especially trying to understand how your background will look when it is being considered through the eyes of an employer. Can you easily identify your transferable skills – that is, those that will directly apply to this job being advertised? What exactly did you do in your last job in terms of practical activities? It is useful to make a preliminary list at this stage to remind yourself how you spent your time in previous jobs. Spend a little time thinking through what went well in these recent jobs, what you achieved, and what key abilities you displayed.

As well as being clear about your strengths and skills, you need to be able to explain away any gaps in your CV, or anything that does not tie up convincingly. For instance, you may have had periods when you were neither employed nor studying. If this is the case, these breaks will likely be noticed and picked up during an interview, so you need to be able to discuss all of your past without embarrassment. This means making the most of the way you have spent your time. If you were unemployed, what did you spend your time doing? If you were traveling, what did you learn from your experiences in different places? Gaps and breaks will not necessarily be seen as bad or regrettable as long as you can talk through what you experienced in a positive light, particularly pointing out what you learned from them.

RESEARCH

The next stage of planning is to collect all the information you can about the vacancy and the organization. You will rarely be invited for an interview without being given some clues as to the sort of candidate required. If the job was advertised and you have been sent a job description or, even better, a person specification, you have as good as been told most of the areas on which you are likely to be questioned.

A job description, as the name suggests, details the main duties of the job and a person specification explains what sort of person the employer is looking for. Both these documents are very useful. Make sure you pay careful attention to all the paperwork that you receive about the job. The employer will have gone through a lot of time and trouble writing down what the post involves. You will be expected to show evidence that you have a lot to offer for every part of it.

Relate your thinking to the research you carried out when initially applying for the post. You need to build on this earlier work and plan out how your background can fit

with the skills and experience that are needed for the
job. If you do not fit the job description or person specification perfectly, find extra points in your favor that could compensate for gaps.

Selling yourself

In the past when applicants for positions were much fewer, carefully working through these documents to show that you had the necessary experience and character would have been enough to get you a job. Nowadays, with so much more competition, it is not just a question of paying attention to detail but of finding ways to 'sell yourself'. Such an expression seems to apply more to washing powder than to human beings, but it is a good term to use.

Consider an advertisement for any washing powder on the television. We are not just shown a box of washing powder and told to buy it. We may be shown a washing line full of sparkling white clothes to demonstrate exactly what the product can do. We are told repeatedly that it washes whiter; gives our clothes a lovely, fresh smell; is substantially cheaper than its rivals; comes in a refillable pack; removes dirt and stains, etc.

Because of all the other advertisements for similar products, the message is hammered home. But when we watch an advert like this, it does not seem as though the message has been too strong; rather, we are left with the impression that it may be a product we ought to try. This is the effect we want to create with the interviewer by using the invited time available to promote our strengths and positive attributes.

Analyzing the job

The job description
By looking closely at the details in the job description you can see what the employer expects the job holder to do. The tasks are sometimes split up into those where some experience is essential and others where experience is preferred. Ideally, you need to go through the following steps:

Work through the job description, taking one section at a time.

Underline or mark the words which mention the main activities of the job (the verbs), eg organizing work; preparing budgets; writing reports; dealing with customers.

Make rough notes to show how you have gained experience in all these activities – think of an example from your background or work experience for each one.

Convert your rough notes into a written or typed form that gives answers to questions on how you satisfy each of the points that you have underlined.

Revisit the information that you provided on your application form, adding more examples as appropriate so that you have a stock of different types of evidence to offer.

Areas of likely questioning

It was stated earlier that an employer will be interested in three main areas of questioning. You know without a doubt that you will be asked questions about (a) your qualifications and skills; (b) your previous work experience; and (c) your character or personality. Let us look at each of these areas in turn.

(a) Your qualifications and skills

Before you are interviewed it is helpful to have prepared a good CV. This document is useful for interviews as well as job applications as it should contain a concise list of courses taken and jobs held. Before the interview, you will need to make a thorough review of your background, especially if you have taken several different courses. Fluffing your answers when you are unsure of your ground is all too apparent to an interviewer and looks unprofessional.

You will then be completely familiar with what you have spent time studying, and where and when. You almost need to be able to recite your CV in your sleep! As a result, when you are asked questions about your educational background, the information you require will come easily and concisely.

When you are being interviewed and are asked about your past studies, the employer does not want to hear you recite a list of the courses you have attended. Think why the employer should be interested in such information. The reason is that he or she wants to know what you learned from your studies. In most cases, therefore, it is more important to get across the main subjects studied, what projects you specifically worked on, which exams you passed – if any – and which parts of the course you enjoyed most, or learned most from.

Those who have not taken any exams will still be expected to talk about courses studied at school or college. You will need to work out which were your favorite subjects, which lessons you felt benefited you most, and why.

Your previous work experience

The same is true of your work experience. All your jobs and the details of what you did as your main duties need to be at the front of your mind. You should not assume that it is obvious to an interviewer what you did as a filing clerk. Most interviewers will be interested in the precise skills used in the job that could help you to contribute to the position applied for.

You may think that all filing clerks file – but what sort of documents were you dealing with? Were they important legal papers or plans, originals of letters, or clients' personal details? Perhaps you used to file things by number rather than alphabetically, or you might have had to cross-reference materials. Did you ever have to retrieve records in a hurry, work under pressure, or trace missing papers? Did you ever use particular IT programs, answer queries from the public or liaise with colleagues from other departments? Were the documents confidential or private or did they need special treatment before filing, eg coding to aid retrieval?

All these things could be what are called transferable skills, ie skills that you learn or use in one job which can be transferred to the next. The advantage to an employer should be obvious. Your skill in one area of work, in which you can demonstrate expertise, means that you will not necessarily need training to do the same thing in the next job.

Again, let us consider why the interviewer is asking this type of question. The answer is, to see what kind of an employee you would make. Therefore, when you worked in a particular place is not as important as what you contributed there, since it gives the employer an idea of your capabilities.

Your character or personality

Of the three main areas of interest to an employer, the greatest importance attaches to the type of person you are. It happens again and again; even if a candidate's educational background or previous experience is not up to those of his or her competitors, by demonstrating certain advantages involving personality or character, the candidate is successful in getting the job. Why should this be so? As long as a candidate is the sort of person who will fit into the company and who enjoys his or her work, that person can easily be trained to compensate for any lack of skills or experience.

Sharing the vision

There is one further aspect for employers to consider when they are interviewing. Many candidates may seem to have appropriate

qualifications, experience, and personality to fit the vacancy. What else could make the difference between the best and the rest? In a downturn, employers may find that they start to attract lots of suitable applicants. They will be looking for ways to pick out the people who are offering them the most. If candidates can show that they have thought about the job, specifically the contribution that they can make and the way that the job should be done, they cannot fail to impress.

This requires spending some time thinking about the key aspects of the job. What are the strengths and weaknesses of the organization as far as you can tell? What can you discover about the environment in which the company is operating? Think about both the job and the organization and try to analyze which factors might be important.

For instance, if the vacancy is with a commercial company, who are its competitors? What is your image of the product or service provided? Are there any changes taking place in the wider world that might affect the company's business? What about the nature of the specific job concerned? What do you see as the most important features of the job and why? How do you imagine yourself doing the job and what special contribution would you make?

Spending time developing your ideas or vision about the future of the organization shows both your commitment to and interest in, the job and the likely added value that you could bring compared to other candidates. Most employers do not have the time to think about the specific details of every job in their organization. They want to recruit people who can do the job well on their behalf and bring fresh ideas and energy to the task. You will enhance the impression you make if you can also talk intelligently about your vision of the organization and how you see your role in i

CHAPTER SIX: DO'S AND DON'TS

DO'S AND DON'TS *IN AN INTERVIEW*

It's no surprise that a strong interview is a determining factor in securing a new position. The more prepared you are, the more confident you will be resulting in a better outcome.

To ensure you put your best foot forward, here are some common faux pas to avoid when facing the pressure of a job interview.

DO: Research the company, check out the website, Facebook page, Twitter feed, and other social media before the interview. How does the company present itself, its workplace culture, and its employees? If the dress code appears to be business casual, then break out your slacks and dress shirt. If it's more formal, then dress the part in traditional business attire from head to foot.

Don't: Dress down. It's better to be slightly more formal than required than to come to the interview dressed too casually, as this gives the appearance that you are not serious about the position. If you're unsure at all, dress better than you think is necessary.

What to Say (without words)

Do: Project confident body language. Sit up straight, lean slightly forward, and look your interviewer in the eye. Smile and engage with each interviewer and nod slightly as he or she speaks.

Don't: Try not to slouch or cross your arms as questions are asked. Don't fidget. Try to project body language that is positive and indicates interest. The best way to show confidence is by sitting in an "open stance". That's why you shouldn't cross your arms or do anything that makes you seem hesitant or closed-off.

How to Act

Do: Stay poised and relaxed. Interviews are designed to see how you react to challenges. That's why so many interviewers try to throw in that one unexpected question. When it comes, be relaxed, flexible, and as engaging as possible. Keep a smile on your face even if you don't have a ready answer. This will show your interviewer that you don't get rattled, even when you don't have all the answers. If you need time to think, say, "That's a great question, let me think for a second. I want to give you a good answer here." No hiring manager is going to fault you for doing that once or twice.

Don't: Don't show signs of panic and don't lose your cool if things take an unexpected turn or you face a tough question. Also, don't rush while answering. You don't want to blurt something out that you can't take back, so stay calm.

When to Hold Back

Do: Let the interviewer feel in control. Let them take the lead and follow the general direction that they're guiding the conversation in. Chances are they have certain things they need to find out from you in order to know if this job is a good fit. And the more you help them gather this info, the better they'll feel about you as a candidate (even if you're missing one or two pieces of experience).

Don't: This doesn't mean you should be completely passive and let it be a one-sided conversation. Don't be afraid to ask the interviewer to clarify something, ask questions midway through the interview, or even go back to a topic you previously discussed if you think of something extra you want to share. So while you don't want to dominate the conversation (remember, the interviewer has topics and questions they *need* to cover), do ask follow-up questions and turn the interview into a dialogue, not just a one-way question-and-answer session.

What to Highlight

Do: Go into your interview prepared to highlight the abilities and the aspects of your background that you believe make you a good fit for the position. Take notes on the position and the company, as well as relevant aspects of your qualifications that make you a strong candidate. Taking the time to research the company and job will help you remember what you want to say, and will allow you to weave your knowledge into the answers to their questions.

Don't: The worst mistake you can make is to skip the pre-interview research stage of preparation. Let's repeat this—the worst mistake you can make is to skip the pre-interview research stage of preparation.

How to Listen

Do: Even though your best strategy is to outline the key points you want to make in the interview ahead of time, you also want to demonstrate that you are a good listener and can stay focused and on topic. Listen to each question as it is asked; you may even want to take notes. Then, calmly and confidently, answer the question in a way that highlights your best attributes.

Don't: Resist the temptation to segue too quickly from the topic of your interviewer's question into your resume. Make sure you tailor your answers in a way that answers the question, stays on topic, and highlights the way your background addresses that topic. If they bring it up then you can bet it's a focus for them, so make sure you demonstrate that it's a focus for you as well.

How to Leverage Your Past

Do: Bring up past successes where appropriate, but make sure that you are constantly showing how these past accomplishments will bring value to your next employer.

Don't: It's tempting to ramble on about your successes in a former job, but do not focus on the specifics of a past role to the point where it dominates the conversation. Remember that even if you loved that former position and learned a
a great deal from it, your next employer is only interested in how that experience will translate into your new role and benefit them.

How to Compensate for Weaknesses

Do: Be honest about elements of your experience or employment record that may not be ideal for the position. If you have gaps in your resume, experienced a layoff or dismissal, or if are missing key experiences or skills in the job description, be truthful, and then leverage the conversation back to your strengths.

Don't: Never lie about past employment missteps or pretend to have skills that you do not have. A good interviewer will see through an attempt to mislead. And even if your lie does get you to the next stage in the hiring process, you're likely to be disqualified later in the vetting process.

How to Talk about Past Employers

Do: Give diplomatic responses about all past employers, even if your tenure at a former job ended badly. Try to find something positive you can say about every past work experience on your resume and then pivot to the skills you have gained along the way that will benefit your next employer.

Don't: You will not win points with your next potential boss by speaking badly of a past one. Even if your past employer is a competitor of the company where you want to work, don't criticize a past employer. You will be seen as petty, or even worse, as a risky hire.

What to Ask

Do: Come prepared with questions based on your research of the company. In addition to checking out the company's website and social media presence, do some industry research and find out some of the innovations or developments your potential employer has gotten noticed for lately. Asking questions indicates your interest in the company, especially when your questions demonstrate knowledge of the industry sector and the company.

Don't: Most interviews end with an opportunity for the candidate to ask about anything that has not previously been covered. But don't wait until the very end of the interview or for the interviewer to ask if you have any questions to ask about the aspects of the job you want to learn more about. Instead, ask questions as the conversation develops and show initiative and confidence. The more you can make the interview into a conversation, the better rapport you'll create with the hiring manager.

How to Wrap Up and Exit

Do: Believe it or not, how you end the interview is just as important as how you begin. In fact, both are crucial, because these are two things that interviewers always remember. So to wrap up your job interview (and our list of interview dos and don'ts), make sure you give a firm handshake, look the interviewer in the eye, and say, "Thanks so much for your time. It was a pleasure meeting you and learning about the role, and I'm looking forward to hearing about the next steps."

You can also ask for a business card so you can call or email the interviewer if they don't provide feedback in a reasonable time frame. Also, consider asking what time frame to expect, so you can plan.

Don't: Make sure you don't rush the ending or leave without thanking them and making eye contact. The last impression matters, and even if you're feeling tense/nervous, or worried that the interview didn't go well, now isn't the time to stress. Focus on what you can control in the moment, which is to leave a good final impression. Also, avoid asking, "Do you have any concerns that would prevent you from offering me the position?" (Or any similar questions).
They just met you and need time to think, and even if they have a big concern, they're not likely to tell you at that moment! It's not a comfortable question to ask, just like the employer wouldn't ask you, "So, are there any reasons you wouldn't accept this job?" I've seen people recommend you ask the

question above, but I don't think it's ever a good idea, and it's one of the biggest interview don'ts. Avoid this, and you'll leave a much better impression.

Always be positive about previous jobs

It is important to always be positive about every job that you have had in the past. Why should this be so vital? Again, let us consider it from the employer's point of view. Will it impress an interviewer to hear a candidate saying what a bad boss his or her last employer was? Will it sound good to hear another company being put down or maligned by a candidate, or will it make the employer think that the

candidates could well be saying the same sort of thing about this company in a few years.

Someone who moans about other organizations also creates an impression of surliness and a negative attitude. Nobody will be interested in employing such a candidate. A candidate who is positive and keen will be preferred.

Be enthusiastic and motivated

Nothing attracts people like enthusiasm. The candidate who exhibits such a characteristic has a great advantage, almost before anything else is said or taken into consideration. We are all more interested in working with the person who comes into work each day in a good mood and feeling positive about the job, rather than with the moaner or troublemaker who is always being negative.

The most common mistakes

- Common mistakes to avoid in an interview

- Arriving at the interview unprepared for what is to follow.

- Having a sloppy appearance or too relaxed an attitude to the interview.

- Not showing any excitement about or enthusiasm for, the work.

- Not seeming to understand the requirements of the job properly.

- Not showing that they have fully considered all aspects of the vacancy, eg indicating a dislike of paperwork when it is clear that this will form a large part of the job on offer.

- Not answering the questions fully and giving answers that are too short.

- Being vague about details and just provide lots of unstructured waffles in their answers.

- Not being clear about their skills and abilities, ie being too vague or modest.

- Seeming overly concerned with what they can get from the job rather than conveying exactly what they are offering

- Using pretentious language or jargon instead of normal speech.

- Do any of these numbered points look familiar to you? Most people have been guilty of one or more of them during interviews. Normally it is feelings of nerves that stop us from coming across at our best. We fail to hear the questions properly; lose the thread of what we are trying to say; totally forget the excellent examples that we prepared to talk about and feel embarrassed about blowing our own trumpet too much.

- Not seeming to understand the requirements of the job properly.

- Not showing that they have fully considered all aspects of the vacancy, eg indicating a dislike of paperwork when it is clear that this will form a large part of the job on offer.

- Not answering the questions fully and giving answers that are too short.

- Being vague about details and just provide lots of unstructured waffles in their answers.
- Not being clear about their skills and abilities, ie being too vague or modest.

- Seeming overly concerned with what they can get from the job rather than conveying exactly what they are offering

- Using pretentious language or jargon instead of normal speech.

- Do any of these numbered points look familiar to you? Most people have been guilty of one or more of them during interviews. Normally it is feelings of nerves that stop us from coming across at our best. We fail to hear the questions properly; lose the thread of what we are trying to say; totally forget the excellent examples that we prepared to talk about and feel embarrassed about blowing our own trumpet too much.

CHAPTER SEVEN: QUESTIONS GUIDE

Brilliant Questions to ask in an interview

Which questions to ask?

At the end of the interview, you will usually be asked if you have any questions to put. Do not feel obliged to ask something just for the sake of it. The employer's heart will sink if you start to reel off a long list of questions just when the interview should be ending. Only ask a question if it is necessary. If you feel that you know all you need to about the job on offer, it is fine to say something like:
'I think that you have covered all the important points already, thank you. But if I have any questions later I will contact you.'
Do not ask questions about uniforms, holidays, or other practical points. If you are offered the post you will be informed about this kind of detail when you start.

If pay has not been mentioned so far, this is not the time to raise the issue. You would probably not accept any position without knowing the wages, but again you can find this out once you receive the offer of the job, when you could reply:

'I am interested in the job at this stage, but I am still not quite sure about the conditions of employment. Can you tell me exactly what the wages and hours are?'

If you do decide to ask the interviewer some questions, it is a good idea to show your general attitude through what you say. Questions about training opportunities or the chance to take on greater responsibilities in the future show that you are keen, plan to stay in the job, and are interested in moving up the organisation.

You could ask: 'Would there be opportunities for more specialist work later on?' or 'Could you tell me a little about what personal development you support for your employees?

The problem, I suspect, is that people worry the invitation to turn the tables is a trap — just another way for interviewers to judge them. They're worried their queries will seem demanding or out of touch, or they wonder if they're supposed to pick questions that will somehow burnish their image as the most highly qualified candidate. Or, especially common, they have no idea how to tactfully ask the things they most want to know. Things like "What are you like as a boss?" and "Is everyone here miserable?"

Questions About the Position

"How will you measure the success of the person in this position?"
This gets right to the crux of what you need to know about the job: What does it mean to do well, and what will you need to achieve for the manager to be happy with your performance?

You may figure the job description has already laid this out, but it's not uncommon for a job description to be the same one an employer has been using for the past ten years, even if the job has changed significantly during that time. Companies often post job descriptions that primarily use boilerplate language from HR, while the actual manager has very different ideas about what's most important in the role. Also, frankly, most employers just suck at writing job descriptions (which is why so many of them sound as if they were written by robots rather than humans), so it's useful to have a conversation about what the role is really about. You may find out that while the job posting listed 12 different responsibilities, your success, in fact, hinges on just two of them, or that the posting dramatically understated the importance of one of them, or that the hiring manager is battling with her boss about expectations for the role, or even that the manager has no idea what success would look like in the job (which would be a sign to proceed with extreme caution).

What are some of the challenges you expect the person in this position to face?
This can elicit the information you'd never get from the job description — like that,

you'll have to deal with messy interdepartmental politics, or that the person you'll be working with most closely is difficult to get along with, or that you'll need to work within draconian budget restrictions on your program.

It can also create an opening for you to talk about how you've approached similar challenges in the past, which can be reassuring to your interviewer. I don't recommend asking questions just so you can follow up with a sales pitch for yourself — that's annoying and usually pretty obvious — but if asking about challenges leads to a genuine discussion of how you'd approach them, it can be useful for you both.

Can you describe a typical day or week on the job?

If the job description mentioned a combination of admin work and program work, it's important to know whether 90 percent of your time will be spent on the admin work or if the split is more like 50/50. Or you might find out that the part of the job that you were most excited about only comes up every six months. Even barring major insights like that, the answer to this question can help you better visualize what it will actually be like to be on the job day after day.

Tip: Some interviewers will respond to this question with, "Oh, every day is different." If that happens, try asking, "Can you tell me what the last month looked like for the person in the job currently? What took up most of their time?"
If nothing you try gets you a clear picture of how your time will be spent, that might be a sign that you'll be walking into chaos — or a job where expectations never get clearly defined.

How long did the previous person in the role hold the position? What has

turnover in the role generally been like?

This is important to ask because if everyone has left the position after less than a year, that could be the sign of a horrible manager, unrealistic expectations, or something else that's likely to make you miserable too. If just one person left quickly, that's not in itself a red flag. But if you find there has been a pattern of quick departures, that should prompt you to ask your interviewer what they think led to the high turnover.
Of course, if the position is brand-new, you can't ask this question. In that case, ask instead about what the turnover on the team has been like.

Questions About Your Success in the Position

What are you hoping this person will achieve in their first six months and their first year?

With this question, you're listening for what kind of learning curve you'll be expected to meet as well as the general pace of the team. If you're expected to have racked up significant achievements in your first, say, six months, you're not going to have a lot of ramp-up time. That may not be a problem if you're coming in with a lot of experience and you know the expectations are reasonable. If not, it may rightly give you pause.

The other advantage of asking this question is that it can elicit details about key projects that you wouldn't otherwise hear about, which can help flesh out your understanding of the work you'll be doing.

In retrospect,can you identify certain traits that separated the people who were successful at this job from those who weren't?

A job candidate asked me this years ago, and it may be the strongest question I've ever been asked in an interview. The thing about this question is that it goes straight to the heart of what the hiring manager is looking for Hiring managers aren't interviewing candidates in the hopes of finding someone who will do an average job; they're hoping to find someone who will shine. And this question says you care about the same thing. Just asking doesn't guarantee that you'll do extraordinary work, but it does make you sound like someone who's at least aiming for that — someone who's conscientious and driven. Those are huge things in a hiring manager's eyes.

Plus, their answer can give you more nuanced insight into what it'll take to truly excel in the job — and whatever the answer is, you can think about whether it's something you'll be able to do.

Questions About the Company

How would you describe the culture here? What type of people tend to thrive here, and what type don't do as well?"

Sometimes hiring managers are pretty bad at accurately describing the culture on their teams — in part because they have a vested interest in seeing it a certain way, and in part because they have an inherently different vantage point than their reports do. For example, I've heard incorrigible micromanagers tell candidates that they like to give people a lot of independence and autonomy. And they probably believed that about themselves! So take managers' descriptions of culture with a heavy grain of salt (and confirm anything important to you with people who are not the manager). That said, there's value in hearing what they do and don't emphasize. You'll often learn what that manager cares about in their employees, which traits will set you up to clash with them, or who's likely to bristle at their management style.

"What do you like about working here?"

You can learn a lot from the way interviewers respond to this question. People who genuinely enjoy their jobs and the company will usually have several things they can cite, and will usually sound sincere. But if you get a blank stare or a long silence before your interviewer answers, or the answer is something like "the paycheck," consider that a red flag.

Ask the question you care about.

It's understandable to want to impress your interviewer, but interviewing is a two-way street — you need to be assessing the job, the employer, and the manager and figuring out whether this is a position you want and would do well in. If you're just focused on getting the job and not on whether it's the right job for you, you're in danger of ending up in a place where you're struggling or miserable.

So before you interview, spend some time thinking about what you really want to know. When you imagine going to the job every day, what are the things that will most impact whether you're happy with the work, with the culture, and with the manager? Maybe it's important to you to work in an informal setting with heavy collaboration. Maybe you care most about working somewhere with sane hours, where calls and texts on the weekend or in the evenings are rare. Maybe you've heard rumors about the stability of the funding for the position and want to see if they're true. Whatever you'll need to know to decide if you want the job, think about asking it now.

That said, you shouldn't take your interviewer's word for it. You should also do due diligence by talking to people in your network who may have the inside scoop on the company's culture or the manager you would be working for, by reading online reviews at places like Glassdoor, and by talking to others who work there. (Here's how to do that.)

"What's your timeline for next steps?"

This is a straightforward logistics question, but it's useful to know when you can expect to hear back. Otherwise, in a few days, you're likely to start agonizing about whether you should have heard back about the job by now and what it means that you haven't, and obsessively check your phone to see if the employer has tried to make contact. It's much better for your quality of life if you know that you're not likely to hear anything for two weeks or four weeks or that the hiring manager is leaving the country for a month and nothing will happen until she's back, or whatever the case might be.

Plus, asking this question makes it easy for you to check in with the employer if the timeline they give you comes and goes with no word. If they tell you that they plan to decide in two weeks and it's been three weeks, you can reasonably email them and say something like, "I know you were hoping to decide around this time, so I wanted to check in and see if you have an updated timeline you can share. I'm interested in the position and would love to talk more with you."

Creating a good Impression

13 great ways to make an impressive impression

First impressions matter, especially in job interviews.

As much as we all wish that actual qualifications mattered most, research suggests that first impressions shape perceptions of professional competence. Those who perform well in the "rapport-building stage" of an interview (when you meet and greet people) are often rated higher on evaluations of professional capabilities, whether or not they are better qualified. Higher ratings lead to more follow-up interviews and eventually more job offers.

So, making a good impression can help you land a job. Here are 13 ways to shine.

Dress for the Job You Want

Dress in professional attire as if you were making an important presentation, meeting with a key client, or having lunch with the senior vice president or CEO.

Make sure your clothes are not too tight, too revealing, or too baggy. If you have a question about whether your attire is inappropriate, don't ask a friend to confirm your choice. Just change your outfit. Also avoid wearing too much jewelry, perfume, or aftershave lotion.

Determining the exact clothing to wear can be tricky as dress codes vary. In many office settings, a suit is the recommended attire. For others, the dress depends on the targeted position, so research (e.g., contact HR, ask a friend who works at the company, and peruse LinkedIn profiles) to decide what to wear, leaning toward classic rather than trendy colors and patterns.

Arrive on Time, but Not Too Early

Ideally, you should arrive about 10-15 minutes before your interview.

Being late for an interview sends the signal that you are unreliable and inattentive to details. Showing up too early makes you seem overeager and stalker-like. If you arrive 30 minutes or more before your scheduled session, then the hiring manager may feel rushed to greet you or uncomfortable with the prospect of having you hang out in a reception area.

Demonstrate promptness without seeming like you have nothing better to do than wait around for a prospective employer. To get the timing right, visit the interview location and determine the appropriate travel time before your meeting day.

Enter a Room Confidently

Your entrance is key to making a positive impression, according to career and professional development advisor Elizabeth

Dexter-Wilson. She recommends keeping your head up, acknowledging those in the room or reception area, smiling, and saying hello.

Offer a Firm Handshake

Shake hands with a firm grip. A firm handshake, not too tight and not at all limp, demonstrates confidence.
Extend your hand in greeting human resource representatives, hiring managers, senior-level managers, and potential colleagues. And, if you are not already standing, stand up when someone enters the room before shaking hands.

Be Kind to Everyone

Show kindness to everyone you meet. You want to make a good first impression in all encounters, not only for kindness' sake but also because those on the front lines may share their perceptions about you with hiring decision-makers.

Be gracious to every person including parking lot attendants, security officers, receptionists, executive assistants, human resources team members, potential co-workers, and hiring managers.

Act Interested

Behave like you are excited about the job, even if you are secretly wondering if the position is a good fit for your talents.

Acting interested can help you engage the interviewers. Then, you can learn more about the organization and its needs, and determine whether you should pursue the position.

Don't Open a Conversation With Careless Remarks

Though most interviewees wouldn't intend to be insulting or insensitive, you might accidentally say something you regret. Avoid conversation starters using too-casual or off-color slang or making comments about personal appearances, politics, religion, or controversial topics.
Plan your opening remarks and be gracious if someone makes an unkind comment to you.

Be Prepared to Talk About the Company and Yourself

Be ready for a conversation with knowledge about the company, responses to common interview questions, and questions of your own.

Don't act like you know everything or you will seem arrogant. But certainly read the organization's website and relevant news so you can talk intelligently about the company.

Practice your responses to typical questions and prepare stories about your recent accomplishments, particularly ones that illustrate how you make you a great fit for the organization. Finally, put together a list of questions to pose when the interviewer asks if you have questions.

Do a Pre-Interview Body Check

Take stock of yourself quickly, beyond your make-up and appearance. Career services professional Barbara Safani recommends three simple actions to prevent distraction and embarrassment:

- remove loose change from your pockets;
- turn off your cell phone;
- toss your cup of coffee or bottle of water.

Check Your Smile

Make sure your smile is nice.
Deal with major issues by visiting a dentist or dental hygienist before you begin the job-search process. On the day of your interview, brush your teeth and floss, and avoid eating right before your meeting.
During the interview, remember to smile.

Carry a Portfolio

You'll want to bring hard copies of your resume, references, and other job-search materials to the interview. Carry these in a portfolio for a polished look.

Know the Answer to *"Why Are You Here?"*

To start your interview well, prepare your response to the question, "Why are you here?"
Note that the response should be more substantial and insightful than "to interview for a job." Tell the interviewer why you are excited about the prospect of joining this particular organization. Briefly explain how your expertise could contribute to the company's success.

Get Your Interviewer's Name Right

Impress your interviewer by getting her name right the first time. This technique is especially helpful if you are meeting someone with an unusual name or if you have difficulty retaining new information. Research the names and titles of those you may be meeting for the first time (hint: look them up on LinkedIn or ask human resources for this information). Rather than ask someone to repeat her name during a face-to-face meeting, memorize the name ahead of time.

CHAPTER EIGHT: PUTTING IT ALL TOGETHER

Step-by-step checklist

Step 1. Planning

To feel confident you need to plan how to convince the employer that you are the best candidate for the position on the day. Get familiar with the job that you will be interviewed for. Collect any helpful information about the company. Go over your application for the post and carefully analyze the specific vacancy to understand what the employer is looking for. The successful candidate will bring out in the interview those examples of his or her background, skills, and personality which complement the ones required for the position. Think about the possible challenges and opportunities of the post to give you a picture of what you would do if offered the position.

The most important point to convey is that you are the right type of person for the job. Study your list of 10 character strengths (see page 98). Select which will be the most useful at the interview. Construct sentences using the points that you have chosen, giving examples of the relevant type of behavior. The details of previous experiences are not as important as your main achievements, the transferable skills learned, or how you behaved. Try to give examples where you can.

Mind the gap! Gaps can be breaks in your employment history or events that you need to convey in a positive light. You need to ensure that you do not sound apologetic about your experiences but can illustrate what you have learned from them. The most important thing about your answers is that they should all be positive – about your previous experience, your skills and strengths, and what makes you right for this particular job.

You can plan your journey; allow extra time to ensure that you arrive at least 15 minutes early for your appointment. There is also some planning work to be done on your physical presentation. Decide which clothes to wear, concentrating on the most flattering style and colors for you. Take professional advice if necessary – a visit to an image consultant can be great fun as well as highly instructive.

Step 2. Preparation

You need to prepare yourself thoroughly for the interview. Do a dummy run of the journey to the organization concerned if it is in an unfamiliar area. A vital part of your preparation concerns the clothes you will wear. They should all be clean, well-ironed, and look immaculate. Have a bath or shower and wash your hair before the interview. Give due consideration to your accessories which can contribute to the employer's important first impression of you. Keep your look plain and simple – don't clutter your appearance too much.

The most vital aspect of the preparatory stage is to speak aloud the answers that you have planned. This rehearses you for the actual performance and increases your confidence when you are asked the questions for real. Think about what the interviewer is going to want to hear from you. You must sound keen and interested in the job; be someone with the right skills or be trainable, and show that you can fit into the organization.

When you are practicing your answers with a friend or in front of the mirror, be aware of how you look and sound. Your voice should be steady and clear. Try to smile while you are talking and see how it improves the way you look and sound. Rehearse your walk; holding yourself up straight can reinforce the impression of confidence as well as making it easier to breathe.

Step 3. Generating confidence

This is the time to let your enthusiasm show. One of the most attractive attributes of a job candidate is a genuine interest in the work. Do not worry about your nerves – just concentrate on enjoying the interview. You are well prepared and confident that you are the right candidate for the job, and you can look forward to meeting the employer and telling him or her about yourself.

Before the event itself, relax your face with the exercise on page 68 and take some deep breaths. Walk in with your head held up, your shoulders well back, and a broad smile to make everyone present feel more at ease. The interviewers are probably quite nervous too and may not be very experienced. Shake hands if you can and remember to thank the interviewer for his or her time when you leave.

Make sure that you speak loudly and fully enough to do justice to your skills and strengths. The employer genuinely wishes to hear what you have to say and only invited you to find out about you, so do not hold back from talking about yourself and your achievements. Imagine that I am there behind you, urging you on to speak up, let your personality out and enjoy the experience. Your path to interview success starts right here. Good luck!

Step 4. Follow-up

It is wise to apply for more than one vacancy at a time, so you always have more interviews ahead of you. Be sure that each one is for a post that interests you though, otherwise, you will not find the motivation to make an impressive application. This helps to keep a sense of perspective about the process and keeps you from feeling demoralized if you don't get a job. It is easy to become depressed about the lack of success in job interviews. However, the most expert interviewees, even those expected to get the job, may be turned down just because, on the day, there happened to be somebody who seemed more suitable.

If you are rejected, it is worth contacting the employer to ask for some feedback on your performance in the interview. Most employers are keen to help as long as the request is phrased politely. I suggest something like:

'I have just attended an interview with you. Although I was not successful, I wondered if I could ask you for any feedback on my performance in the interview, as I am particularly interested in this type of work and your comments might help me in the future.'

Another antidote to feeling despondent about searching for work is to mix with other people in the same situation. A supportive group can keep you going when you feel at the end of your tether. At times you will need to fight the feeling that there is something wrong with you as a person. Sharing your experiences with other people will remind you that other excellent candidates fail to get jobs. Maintaining some semblance of a work routine is also helpful in keeping up morale. Voluntary work, for example, provides contacts, experience, and a sense of purpose and self-worth. Some kind of study or training keeps you developing, gives you the chance to interact with others, and can prove to be very rewarding.

The Government's New Deal program may be available if you are out of work. Contact your local Jobcentre Plus to join the scheme and use their facilities, expertise, and contacts. Visit www.jobcentreplus.gov.uk for more details.

If you keep getting invited to interviews then you know that your written applications are of a high standard. If you keep attending interviews, always doing your best, and trying to improve, you will eventually get a job. Strongly resist feeling demoralized, depressed, or unconfident. It was said earlier that interviews should be treated as learning experiences. Even if you are not successful at an interview, you can feel pleased in the knowledge that you have done your best to create a good impression.

Step 5. Learning from experience

Whenever you attend an interview make a note immediately afterward of the questions you were asked and how you replied. Try to get the wording down exactly too. Evaluate what happened. Did any of the questions take you by surprise? If so, they need fuller preparation next time. Which of your answers seemed to go down well? Why was that? Which answers would you change with hindsight? How do you feel you could have improved these answers? Could you have been more positive, spoken more fully, or given more examples? If you were unsuccessful and you get feedback from the employer, to improve on your areas of weakness. You might need to get additional information, practice more, or spend extra time focusing on how you fit with the next vacancy you go for. This exercise will prove very useful if you ever go for a similar vacancy, or apply to the same organization in the future. It is also helpful to reflect on afterward. Continuous improvement comes from looking back and learning in this way.

CHAPTER NINE: QUESTIONS AND ANSWERS

common interview questions and answers.

So, you landed an interview! Congratulations—that's no small feat. Getting an interview is an incredible feeling, but it can also be a stressful experience. You want to be 100% prepared when you walk through the door or turn on that video chat. Today, we'll prepare you for your interview by reviewing the most common interview questions and answers. And don't worry if you lack relevant experience. In this article, you'll find advice that's tailored to new college graduates and early-career job seekers.

Before we get to the questions, let's review a few interview basics:

Be sure to bring extra copies of your resume, cover letter, and work samples to the interview.

Do your research beforehand. Review the company website, local business news sites, and your interviewer's LinkedIn profile.

Arrive a few minutes early to show that you're reliable.

During the interview, listen carefully, stay on topic, and use the STAR method. Be positive and enthusiastic, no matter what.

Send a thank-you note within 48 hours of the interview. If you don't hear back, wait at least two weeks before following up about the next steps.

Now, onto the top interview questions and answers:

What are your strengths?
What is your greatest weakness?
Tell me about yourself.
Why do you want to work here?
Where do you see yourself in five years?
Why should we hire you?
Why did you apply for this position?
Do you prefer to work on a team or independently?

What type of work environment do you prefer?
How do you deal with pressure or stressful situations?
What are your hobbies?
Do you have prior experience?
Who was the most difficult person you ever worked with?
How would your professors/friends/co-workers describe you?
Do you have any questions for me?

What are your strengths?

Don't look at this common interview question as a trick, but rather a gift. This question provides an excellent opportunity for you to demonstrate your personality, expertise, and preparation for the interview.

Choose two or three strengths that reflect you and are directly related to the job. Then, support at least one of them with evidence, such as awards, metrics, or specific anecdotes. Stay away from clichés and focus on substantive answers. The interviewer is looking for quality, not quantity. Here's a good response:

I believe one of my greatest strengths is time management. For example, last semester I managed to earn a 3.8 GPA while working 20 hours a week at a local coffee shop, serving as president of my fraternity, and acting as a teaching assistant for a freshman writing course. I'm also very organized and detail-oriented.

What is your greatest weakness?

The key to nailing this dreaded job interview question is to not let it psych you out. When it comes to your greatest weakness, the hiring manager is not as concerned with what you say as how you say it. They're looking for honesty and confidence, so watch your body language and maintain eye contact.

Always give an example of how you're attempting to strengthen your area of weakness when responding, and prepare your response in advance. For instance, because I'm a very organized person, I have a hard time with ambiguity and last-minute changes. For school, I planned out every assignment, but in the workplace, priorities, and deadlines are always shifting.

I'm attempting to adapt to those changes more as a result. My online project management course has shown me how to adjust to changing priorities. I now understand how to reorder my priorities in the event of an unforeseen changes.

Tell me about yourself.

An interview frequently begins with this standard opening question. Additionally, interviewees frequently make mistakes by either saying too much or not enough. Just show the highlights; hiring managers don't want to hear about your entire life. Share your career highlights and significant achievements to demonstrate how you will contribute to the position. Try to establish a personal connection with the interviewer while also expressing your enthusiasm for the position.

You don't have to limit your answers to work and school; this is not the case with most interview questions. Mentioning your interests or accomplishments is acceptable as well. To put it another way, this question is ideal for people who have little to no work experience. You want to leave a lasting impression on your interviewer, so demonstrate your versatility. One possible response is:

Although most people have never heard of the small town where I grew up in upstate New York, I'm sure you'll recognize it because it was listed as your hometown in your employee bio. How small the world is. I moved here a year ago after receiving my degree from ABC University to work as an executive assistant at XYZ Organization. It complimented my love of analytics and developing creative campaigns well. My search for my next professional challenge is currently in progress, and I think I've found it at your business.

Why do you want to work here?

Take this query as a request to share your research and company knowledge. Make it clear to the hiring manager that you have done your research and are genuinely interested in working only here. Focus on how your skills, objectives, and beliefs line up with the company as you discuss the specifics that attracted you to the company.

The dedication of your business to the neighborhood is one of the main reasons I want to work here. It distinguishes you from your rivals. I adore the fact that each spring you all volunteer at the Special Olympics. I've worked with the neighborhood every week for the previous four years at an animal shelter. I place a lot of importance on working for a company that also emphasizes helping others.

Where do you see yourself in five years?

Interviewers ask you this question to learn more about you, but they're also thinking about the company's interests. The fact is, it takes a lot of time and money to find new hires and train them. The interviewer, therefore, wants to make sure that you are committed to them and in it for the long run. They also want to know that your expectations are reasonable. Although having lofty goals is acceptable, stating that you plan to hold a vice president position in five years is a red flag.

An excellent response should allay the employer's concerns. Inform them that you intend to stay with the business. Then, by outlining your specific career objectives and desire to advance within the organization, you can demonstrate your diligence

and ambition. Find more senior employees at the company with the titles you're interested in using websites like LinkedIn. Here's an illustration:

I envision myself working at XYZ Company for five years, contributing to the team and enhancing the branch. I appreciate that you provide so many chances for professional growth, and I want to advance with the business. I therefore intend to become an assistant expert in the upcoming years, and then hopefully advance to associate.

Why should we hire you?

This interview question is open-ended, so you should approach it in two ways: You should start by emphasizing the qualities or experiences that make you special. Second, you should demonstrate how the company will benefit from the uniqueness.

Make sure to emphasize qualities that would make you a great fit for the company culture to distinguish yourself from the competition. Another instance in which thoroughly researching the topic and showing genuine enthusiasm can have a significant impact. Here's a good illustration:

In the world of advertising, ABC Company is admired for its dedication to originality. I've taken pride in being a creative person ever since I can remember. I oversaw the organization of more than a dozen various, themed events for my sorority in college last year. The sorority typically hosts five events each year. I'm eager to consider how my imagination and ambition might improve on what is already excellent here.

Why did you apply for this position?

Hiring managers are essentially asking, "Have you done your research and do you know what this specific job entails?" in this situation. This is about your role, as opposed to "Why do you want to work here?" which is about the company. And for this particular question, you must carefully craft your response. Keeping the job description in mind is the best way to stay on course.

Mention the main objectives, demands, and tasks that resonate with you. Then, emphasize how the position fits your skill set and career goals perfectly. Don't bring up money, one more thing. Even if you applied for this job primarily to pay the bills, you shouldn't admit it (or even make a joke about it). An emphatic response could be:

I'm a seasoned author who genuinely enjoys what she does. And I'm looking for a chance to put my excellent writing and editing abilities to use to create compelling messages. Because it will let me exercise my writing skills and work on a variety of projects at once, I was especially drawn to the cross-industry

clients you support. While I anticipate it will be busy, I also anticipate it to be exciting.
Do you favor working alone or in a group?
There is no right or wrong response in this situation, but tactfulness is advised. It's critical that your response amply demonstrates your versatility, whether you're an extrovert or an introvert. While expressing your preference, keep in mind the particulars of the role. Hopefully, you enjoy working with people if you organize events.
Include two successful examples in your response: one in which you worked well with a team and the other in which you performed well on a solo project.
I adore team projects. There were problems with a few of my fellow interns not getting

along when I interned with XYZ Company. I stepped in and planned a social event for the group, which really assisted them in putting their differences aside. We worked together to come up with the best ideas to end the summer on a great note. I also like working alone when it's necessary, though. I was proud of myself in school for never missing an essay deadline. That was possible because I can concentrate by lowering my head.

What type of work environment do you prefer?

Make sure that your response fits with the company's culture and reputation, regardless of how you choose to respond to this question. Therefore, make sure to conduct preliminary research. If the company you're interviewing with is known for its relaxed, chill environment, for instance, you don't want to say you like a fast-paced work environment.

Give an example of a preference you believe the interviewer will value based on the research you've done on the company's website and Glassdoor reviews. Avoid saying or doing anything that could be seen as a negative reflection on you (everyone wants two-hour lunch breaks; don't tell anyone). Here's an illustration:

My ideal workplace places a high value on employee input and communication. I'm aware that interested employees gather for lunch on Fridays at XYZ Company once a month, and I enjoy that. Transparency and communication are very important to me as well.

How do you deal with pressure or stressful situations?

The reason hiring managers adore this interview question is that it enables them to confirm that: 1) You have dealt with stressful events in the past, and 2) You will be able to deal with stressful situations while working for their organization. Honesty and setting a good example are essential to generating a positive impression.

Prepare a strong example of how you've handled pressure or stressful situations in the past in advance of the interview. Stay optimistic while being honest. As long as you are trying to get better, it's acceptable if you have trouble under pressure. Additionally, don't act as though you are always composed and can handle any pressure. Here's an illustration:

I try my hardest to maintain composure and concentrate on a solution in stressful situations. For instance, I occasionally had authors miss deadlines when I served as the feature editor of my undergraduate newspaper. Instead of freaking out, I took a

calm approach and wrote the pieces myself. Later, I met with each writer
individually, and together, we devised a strategy to ensure that didn't occur again. Because we had dealt with the root of the problem, I eventually never had to experience that kind of stress again.

Additionally, avoid giving off the impression that you are constantly calm because that could come across as overconfident or even misleading as someone who is only trying too hard to get the job.

What are your hobbies?

Don't think too much about this query. Managers of hiring don't use it to trip you up. Instead, they genuinely want to ensure that you have the right personality for their business. Once more, the best course of action is honesty. If you say something you think is impressive, like that karate is one of your hobbies, you don't want to find out later that the hiring manager is a black belt and wants to know more about your dojo because you didn't tell the truth.

Unless you're applying for a job where you know such answers are appropriate, stay away from anything political, religious, or that could have a negative connotation (like gambling). Just mention two or three activities that demonstrate your dedication and demonstrate that you have a life outside of work. For instance:

Running is one of my favorite pastimes. Every day I try to run, and I complete about ten 5K races annually. It facilitates my ability to unwind and think clearly. Running is one of my favorite ways to raise money for causes I care about, like the Humane Society. I enjoy spending time with my two rescue dogs because they are such fun.

Do you have prior experience?

Do not be alarmed by this question. It's unlikely that you've ever held a job exactly like the one you're interviewing for if this is your first job after college. You do, however, know! Share any pertinent experience you've gained through your studies, volunteer work, side jobs, internships, and extracurricular activities.
It gives your response more credibility if you can describe your prior successes with specific outcomes and metrics. Don't rely solely on your academic performance, though. Your practical experience is of greater interest to the hiring manager.

I have prior experience in the field of research, yes. I worked as an intern at ABC Lab for eight semesters while in college. I co-authored two papers there that were eventually published.

**Who was the most difficult person
you ever worked with**?

Be very cautious when answering this
question. In your new position, you'll work
with a lot of people, and you won't get along
with everyone. However, you'll still need to
collaborate effectively.
The "who" in this sentence is unimportant;
in any case, avoid mentioning anyone by
name. Instead, the interviewer is interested
in learning how you were able to cooperate
with this person despite the challenges.
After all, if you've previously
resolved a difficult working relationship,
you can do it again. Avoid being petty, and
make sure to wrap things up well.
Last year, I worked with a challenging lab
partner. He was disorganized, and because
he didn't keep me informed of his
development, we kept missing deadlines. To
stay on track, I eventually insisted on
weekly in-person check-ins. He initially
found it annoying, but we eventually

finished the task, and we parted ways amicably.

How would your professors/friends/co-workers describe you?

If you haven't given this question any thought beforehand, it may be difficult. Think about recent feedback you've gotten, both good and bad. The main objective of the interviewer is to make sure you have a clear understanding of how others perceive you and how your actions affect them. Consider providing two positive characteristics and one area for improvement in your response to demonstrate your self-awareness. For instance:

I'm the president of the student council, so the other members might say that I'm a really good leader. I was also given the moniker "Mr. Congeniality" because I get along well with everyone. However, they would also claim that I occasionally take on too many tasks at once. I'm attempting to delegate more.

Do you have any questions for me?

A word of caution: This is essentially a given question that could make or break the relationship. So, be ready.
This is your last chance to make a strong impression on the hiring manager. Bring a list of prepared questions to the interview. Since many will be addressed during the interview, we advise having at least 10 prepared. If
Better yet, you can think of questions right away based on what you learned from the interview.
Last but not least, never assert that "Nope, you covered everything." Not asking any questions demonstrates a lack of

preparation, interest, and participation in the interview. To help you get started, consider these excellent questions:

You mentioned that ABC Company offers a variety of opportunities for ongoing professional development. Can you elaborate on these for me?

What do you want me to achieve in the first 60 days? before the year is over?

Can you describe a typical day in this position for me?

 We don't say this to frighten you. Instead, it ought to motivate and inspire you. You'll be able to reflect on your interview and know that it helped you land your dream job if you go into it with the right mindset and preparation.
Practice the aforementioned 15 questions first. Then, it comes down to being confident and sincere. Present your best self to the hiring manager, and demonstrate that you have done your research. Their

choice will be simple thanks to you, and
naturally favorable to you.

CONCLUSION

"The Art of Mastering Interviews" is a comprehensive guide that equips readers with the knowledge and skills needed to excel in any interview setting. Throughout the book, we have explored various facets of the interview process, from preparation to execution, and provided practical tips and strategies for success.

By delving into the mindset of both the interviewer and the interviewee, we have uncovered the key factors that contribute to a successful interview.

Ultimately, this book aims to instill in readers the confidence and self-assurance necessary to leave a lasting impression on interviewers. It is not just a guide for acing interviews, but a valuable resource that can be referred to time and again throughout one's career.

So, whether you are a recent graduate preparing for your first interview or a seasoned professional looking to enhance your interview skills, "The Art of Mastering

Interviews" offers practical guidance and expert advice to help you achieve your goals. With the knowledge gained from this book, you will be well-equipped to confidently tackle any interview and secure the job of your dreams.

www.ingramcontent.com/pod-product-compliance
Lightning Source LLC
Chambersburg PA
CBHW070939260726
48661CB00003B/1035